DISSENT AND STRATEGIC LEADERSHIP OF THE MILITARY PROFESSIONS

Don M. Snider

February 2008

This publication is a work of the U.S. Government as defined in Title 17, United States Code, Section 101. As such, it is in the public domain, and under the provisions of Title 17, United States Code, Section 105, it may not be copyrighted.

*****

An early version of this monograph was presented October 15, 2007, at a conference in Washington, DC, sponsored by the Foreign Policy Research Institute (*www.fpri.org*) and The Reserve Officers Association (*www.roa.org*).

*****

The views expressed in this report are those of the author and do not necessarily reflect the official policy or position of the United States Military Academy, Department of the Army, the Department of Defense, or the U.S. Government. This report is cleared for public release; distribution is unlimited.

*****

Comments pertaining to this report are invited and should be forwarded to: Director, Strategic Studies Institute, U.S. Army War College, 122 Forbes Ave, Carlisle, PA 17013-5244.

*****

All Strategic Studies Institute (SSI) publications are available on the SSI homepage for electronic dissemination. Hard copies of this report also may be ordered from our homepage. SSI's homepage address is: *www.StrategicStudiesInstitute.army.mil*.

*****

FOREWORD

Over the past 5 years, the War on Terrorism has produced many unforeseen results for the U.S. Army, something not unexpected by those who study war as we do here at the Strategic Studies Institute (SSI). One event, however, was truly unexpected—the participation in 2006 by several Army flag officers in the "Revolt of the Generals."

It was unexpected because the professional ethic of the Army in the modern era has held that, in civil-military relations, the military is the servant of its Constitutionally-mandated civilian leaders, both those in the Executive branch and in the Congress. Thus, as Samuel Huntington noted over 5 decades ago, "loyalty and obedience" are the cardinal military virtues. This precept has remained embedded in the Army's professional ethos to this day, especially for the strategic leaders of the Army Profession. An act of public dissent is to be exceptionally rare, undertaken only after the most careful analysis and determination of its absolute necessity.

While much of the commentary on the "Revolt" has focused on whether it was right, or even legal, for these officers to dissent from the policies and leadership of the Rumsfeld-led Pentagon, the author of this monograph, Dr. Don Snider, develops a different framework, a moral framework, with which to analyze the event. Drawing on his extensive background in the study of the U.S. Army as a profession, Dr. Snider isolates the three critical trust relationships which enable the Army to be, and to behave as, a social trustee profession empowered to apply its expert knowledge in defense of America and her interests. He then develops indicators by which those considering dissent should analyze the potential costs to the profession emanating from impacts on these critical trust relationships.

Not surprisingly, Dr. Snider concludes that effective stewardship of the profession by the current strategic leaders of the Army has been made more difficult by the Revolt. Further, he recommends that they refurbish and uphold the profession's traditional ethic on public dissent as a means of reasserting control over critical jurisdictions of the profession.

We are pleased to publish this work, completed while Dr. Snider was at SSI on sabbatical from West Point during the fall of 2007. It extends and complements an earlier work completed here on another short sabbatical in 2004, *The Future of the Army Profession*, 2d Edition, coedited with Lloyd J. Matthews.

DOUGLAS C. LOVELACE, JR.
Director
Strategic Studies Institute

BIOGRAPHICAL SKETCH OF THE AUTHOR

DON M. SNIDER is a Professor of Political Science at the United States Military Academy. He is a retired Colonel, U.S. Army, with three combat tours in Vietnam, service on the Army and Joint Staffs, and on the staff of the National Security Council, the White House. Dr. Snider's teaching and research focus at West Point is on the American political system, civil-military relations, the role of military professions, and the development of commissioned officers. His most recent publications, both coedited with Lloyd J. Matthews, are: *The Future of the Army Profession*, 2d Edition, (2005) and *Forging the Warrior's Character: Moral Precepts from the Cadet Prayer* (2007).

SUMMARY

Vice Admiral James Stockdale, Vietnam prisoner of war and Medal of Honor recipient, once said, "Even in the most detached duty, we warriors must keep foremost in our minds that there are boundaries to the prerogatives of leadership, moral boundaries."

In this monograph, the author delineates a segment of these boundaries as they are understood from the study of military professions and as derived from the roles and responsibilities of those seniors privileged to be the profession's temporary stewards—the colonels/captains and Flag Officers who comprise the strategic leadership. Such boundaries mean that the decision to dissent can never be a purely personal matter. Rather it will reverberate outward impinging at a minimum the three critical trust relationships of the military profession—those with the American people, those with civilian and military leaders at the highest levels of decisionmaking, and those with the junior corps of officers and noncommissioned officers of our armed forces.

To analyze the impact of dissent on these three critical trust relationships, the author isolates five different but closely related aspects of public dissent that should be considered by the strategic leader when deciding whether to take such a step—the gravity of the issue; the relevance of the professional's expert knowledge and expertise to the issue at question; and, the three indicators of the dissenter's motive—the personal sacrifice to be incurred in dissenting; the timing of the act of dissent; and the congruence of such an act with the previous career of service and leadership within the military profession. None of these five factors by themselves will likely be determinative for the would-be dissenter, but collectively they provide a moral context and framework in which a judgmental decision should be made.

The author concludes that if, as a result of these considerations the military leader decides that dissent is warranted—if the leader believes that an act of dissent best balances the immediate felt obligation to bring his/her professional military expertise to bear in a public forum with the longer-term obligation to lead and represent the profession as a social trustee, as a faithful servant of the American people, and as expressly subordinate to civilian control—then for those rare instances there should be no additional restrictions placed on any act of dissent. On rare occasions, true professionals must retain the moral space to "profess."

He also concludes that what remains now is for the strategic leaders of the military profession to strongly promote and follow the existing professional ethic, reinforcing a culture that discourages public dissent because of the risks to the profession's essential trust relationships. He maintains that this will be no easy task for the current leaders, but it is an urgent one—reasserting that they alone fulfill the functional roles of representing the profession, rendering advice, and executing legal orders. They must make it abundantly clear that they and they alone, speak for the military profession. All other military voices, including those retired, are heard from nonpracticing professionals and should be considered as such. This will require reestablishing control over their profession's certification processes to ensure that all parties to civil-military relations understand that retired officers speak for no one other than themselves as citizens; and, most notably, that they do not speak for the current practicing professionals who now lead in America's conflicts.

DISSENT AND STRATEGIC LEADERSHIP OF THE MILITARY PROFESSIONS

> The U.S. military has a long tradition of strong partnership between the civilian leadership of the Department of Defense and the uniformed services. Both have long benefited from a relationship in which the civilian leadership exercises control with the advantage of fully candid professional advice, and the military serves loyally with the understanding that its advice has been heard and valued. That tradition has been frayed, and civil-military relations need to be repaired.[1]
>
> *Iraq Study Group Report*, December 2006

> Personal and professional honor do not require request for reassignment or retirement if civilians order one's service, command, or unit to act in some manner an officer finds distasteful, disastrous, or even immoral. The military's job is to advise and then execute lawful orders. . . . If officers at various levels measure policies, decisions, orders, and operations against personal moral and ethical systems, and act thereon, the good order and discipline of the military would collapse.[2]
>
> Professor Richard H. Kohn, 2007

INTRODUCTION

The two epigraphs above establish the scope of this monograph. For a number of well-known reasons, all much discussed within the military and in the press, academic conferences, and journals, civil-military relations in America during the Iraq War have been filled with tensions, or "frayed" in the words of the Iraq Study Group. Often these tensions manifested themselves in notably controversial behavior by either civilian or military leaders, behavior seemingly at odds with patterns we have come to expect from past experiences. Conspicuous among these behaviors is what has become known as "The Revolt of the Generals," when several senior flag officers, all retired, spoke out publicly in 2006 against both the military policies pursued in Iraq and the civilian leaders (Secretary of Defense Donald Rumsfeld *et al.*) who were most responsible for them.[3]

Now, with the departure of Secretary Rumsfeld and many of the civilian leaders and military flag officers he put in place, and abetted by a change in strategy that may at long last be advancing the counterinsurgency effort, such tensions and dissenting behaviors have somewhat ebbed. However, as the second epigraph demonstrates, strong feelings and opinions still linger about this period in American civil-military relations, and, more specifically, about the appropriateness of the "Revolt" and its reverberating influences on America's military and political cultures. It is not a stretch to note that these reactions are intensifying with time.[4] This monograph, then, will focus on the subject of military dissent using the revolt as a stimulus for thinking more clearly about this latest phase in the Republic's civil-military relations.

First, it is necessary to describe the revolt. I speak of the behavior of six retired general officers who, in various manners and public forums and for somewhat similar reasons, broke their services' traditions in early 2006 to speak out during war against their civilian leaders and the war policies they represented. These were, incidentally, policies which earlier the general officers themselves had each helped to formulate or execute. Of interest to this monograph are not the differences among the rationales they each offered for their public dissent, rather we are interested in the common theme, one most clearly expressed by Lieutenant General Gregory Newbold, U.S. Marine Corps (USMC), whose April 2006 article in *Time* magazine was hyped as "a full-throated" critique. Here are the key excerpts:

> After 9/11 [September 11, 2001], I was a witness and therefore party to the actions that led us to the invasion of Iraq—an unnecessary war. Inside the military family, I made no secret of my view that the zealots' rationale for war made no sense. And I think I was outspoken enough to make those senior to me uncomfortable. But I now regret that I did not more openly challenge those who were determined to invade a country whose actions were peripheral to the real threat—al Qaeda. I retired from the military 4 months before the invasion, in part because of my opposition to those who had used 9/11's tragedy to hijack our security policy. Until now, I have resisted speaking out in public. I've been silent long enough.
>
> I am driven to action now by the mistakes and misjudgments of the White House and the Pentagon, and by my many painful visits to our military hospitals. . . . With the encouragement of some still in positions of military leadership, I offer a challenge to those still in uniform: a leader's responsibility is to give voice to those who can't—or don't—have the opportunity to speak. . . .
>
> What we are now living with is the consequence of successive policy failures. . . . Flaws in our civilians is one thing: the failure of the Pentagon's military leaders is quite another. Those are the men who know the hard consequences of war but, with few exceptions, acted timidly when their voices urgently needed to be heard. When they knew the plan was flawed, saw intelligence distorted to justify a rationale for war, or witnessed arrogant micromanagement that at times crippled the military's effectiveness; many leaders who wore the uniform chose inaction. A few of the most senior officers actually supported the logic for war. Others were simply intimidated, while still others must have believed that

the principle of obedience does not allow for respectful dissent....[5]

The revolt occurred for what each officer felt were principled reasons flowing, essentially, from policy differences☐ wrong war; wrong place; not well-planned, resourced, or executed; and culpable civilian leaders not replaced. True, several did mention other concerns such as the management style of civilian leaders, Secretary Rumsfeld in particular. But I believe all of the dissenters to be forthright men without ulterior motives, and that their main issue was substantive with respect to war policy.[6]

Granting that military professions, and their ethics in particular, do evolve slowly over time and that this revolt was an aberration when viewed against the historical pattern of military ethics in the U.S. military, the broad question for this monograph becomes whether the professions☐ ethics should evolve to accommodate in the future the forms of military dissent expressed in this instance? Or should they evolve in ways that continue, as they have in the past, to strongly discourage such public dissent by uniformed leaders, active and retired, during wartime?

Further, since the slow evolution of military ethics is most influenced by the stewards entrusted with its maintenance☐ the strategic leaders of the military professions☐ we are also interested in the role of military dissenters as strategic leaders. Stated another way, since the ethic of the military profession is at any point in time the result of the leadership (decisions and actions) of previous strategic leaders, how are we to think about the influences of dissenting behavior on the evolution of the profession, its professionals, and their ethic?

I will approach these contentious questions in three steps:
- First, I shall present from the literature the various forms of military dissent being discussed so that all readers can understand the full range of actions available to those who chose to dissent. I will do this primarily by reference to recent work by colleagues that uses a two-factor analysis to focus on a policy-content rationale for analyzing and explaining the range of potential acts of military dissent.
- Second, I will look at an alternative approach, one that draws on the nature of military professions and their ethics of trust to analyze the various influences dissent can have on those trust-based relationships. This approach goes beyond the narrow issue of whether the war policies of civilian leaders are sound, dealing instead with the broader issue of whether such public dissent irrespective of the substantive correctness of the dissent is ultimately healthy for the profession, its professionals, and its ethic.
- Last, I will offer some concluding observations on events now lying over the horizon.

Before we proceed, however, I must note a fundamental consensus on at least one point that over-watches our inquiry. That is the concept of civilian control or, perhaps more precisely, democratic political control of the military in America. The U.S. military is subordinate to the President and to certain designated officials in the Executive branch as well as to elected political leaders in Congress. According to the U.S. Constitution, these two branches of the federal government share primary authority and responsibility for military affairs. The military is, therefore, the servant of its Constitutionally-mandated masters and through them, the citizens of the Republic. A desirable pattern of U.S. civil-military relations, including legitimate military dissent, would therefore enhance democratic political control while also facilitating sound strategic decisionmaking and the creation of effective military institutions.[7]

Despite a broad consensus on this fundamental point, there is nevertheless plenty of room for disagreement on many subordinate issues, including, as we shall see, military dissent.

PART I: A FRAMEWORK FOR THOUGHT

In an opinion piece posted on the website of the Strategic Studies Institute, U.S. Army War College, Professors Leonard Wong and Douglas Lovelace portray in the schema below the options available to officers when considering acts of dissent. This schema applies to the policy formulation stage, before a decision is finally made and promulgated:[8] To Wong and Lovelace, the important considerations clearly lie in the policy environment, the degree of resistance civilian leaders display to the military's professional expertise and advice, and the importance to the nation's security of the issue being debated.

According to these scholars, the hard choices, those in which strong action is appropriate, lie in the upper right quadrant where both resistance and the threat are more serious, i.e., situations like the Iraq War. Note that Wong and Lovelace present the full spectrum of choices available to officers, ranging from mere

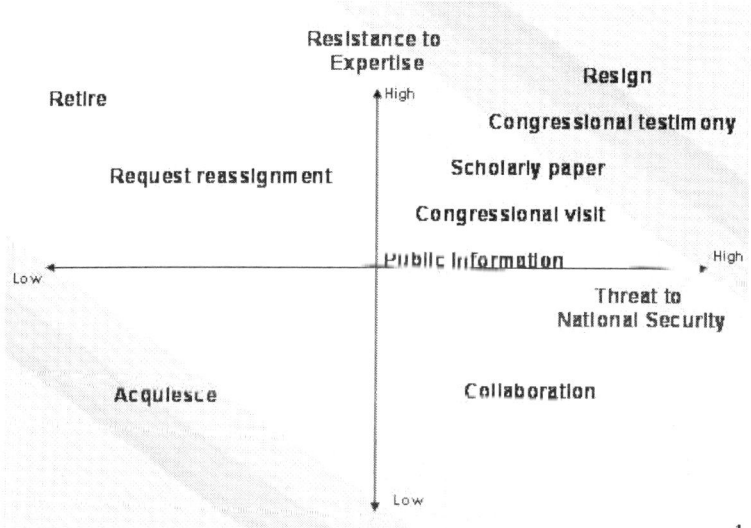

acquiescence to the policy in question up to the most costly act of dissent, resignation of one's commission which includes forfeiture of retirement and all other benefits that go with it.

However, are the two variables portrayed in the schema—policy content and relationships at the civil-military nexus—all that the strategic leaders of America's military profession should consider when contemplating dissent? Or do they have other equally important responsibilities that should bring into play additional variables or considerations? That is to say, are there other responsibilities derivable from their status as leaders of a social trustee profession whose lifeblood is the public's perception of the trustworthiness of the practitioners?

PART II: WHAT ARE THE CHARACTERISTICS OF MILITARY PROFESSIONS AND THEIR ETHIC OF TRUST; WHAT ARE THE FACTORS WITHIN DISSENT THAT CAN STRENGTHEN OR WEAKEN CRITICAL TRUST RELATIONSHIPS?[9]

Before considering a model of modern, competitive military professions and their requisite ethical behavior, we should note that the ethic of military professions has both legal and moral components. On commissioning, officers of America's military professions swear by a legally binding oath that they will do certain things and behave in certain ways, and then serve according to the standards of the Uniformed Code of Military Justice (UCMJ) which provides for various legal sanctions in case of violations of that Code, violations demonstrating a failure to fulfill one's duties as prescribed.[10]

But the legal code is not of primary interest in this inquiry. Retired officers, unlike active duty officers, can speak freely and, except in the rarest of cases, not be prosecuted for such actions under UCMJ.[11] The question for this inquiry is not whether they are *entitled* to speak freely; but, whether they *should* ? Thus we are more interested here in the implied moral aspects of the profession's ethic than in its legal aspects.

That said, however, there is one particular in which the legally codified aspects of the professions' ethics does have bearing on our inquiry. Specifically, in the United States Code, Title 10, Armed Forces (Sections 3583, 85831, and 5947), "Requirements of Exemplary Conduct" establishes as a matter of law the commander's responsibility for the moral and ethical stewardship of his/her unit, to wit:

> All commanding officers and others in authority in the [Army/Air Force, naval service] are required:
>
> (1) to show themselves as a good example of virtue, honor, patriotism, and subordination;
>
> (2) to be vigilant in inspecting the conduct of all persons who are placed under their command;
>
> (3) to guard against and suppress all dissolute and immoral practices, and to correct, according to the laws and regulations of the Army, all persons who are guilty of them, and;
>
> (4) to take all proper and necessary measures, under laws, regulations, and customs of the Army, to promote and safeguard the morale, the physical well being, and the general welfare of the officers and the enlisted persons under their command or charge (brackets added).[12]

It is of interest to note, therefore, that all commissioned officers, and particularly those in the chain of command, are expected to be at all times "a good example of virtue, honor, patriotism, and subordination." This includes retired military professionals so long as they have never resigned their commission. But what is such a "good example," and how are we to think about it and evaluate alternative forms of dissent in the context of this legal and moral requirement for "subordination" and the related qualities mandated by the commissioning oath? To help us in that regard, we turn now to a brief review of modern competitive professions, particularly the military professions.

Modern Competitive Professions.[13]

We can fairly say that all societies generally organize their productive work under one of three ideal models: business, bureaucracy, or profession.[14] In this context, our armed forces are producing institutions: for example, the Army produces "the human expertise, embodied in leaders and their units, of effective land combat.[15] In the first model, businesses generally operate within the interactions of markets, with economic forces producing the motivating rationale. Most all inputs are organized into markets (labor, capital, technology, etc.) from which businesses acquire the wherewithal to produce something of use and value for consumers. Under various levels of regulation or oversight, markets will equilibrate to a price and quantity of production that satisfies suppliers, producers, and consumers. Thus, economic profit and productive efficiency are the motivating forces within this type of productive activity. And the resulting arms-length relationship between producer and consumer has long been aptly characterized in economic texts as *caveat emptor,* or "let the buyer beware."

In contrast to a business, a bureaucracy does not operate on economic or market incentives at all. Rather, efficiency in repetitive production processes is the main guiding principle of bureaucratic institutions, which tend to operate in their own interest for their self-perpetuation. Some degree of bureaucracy is intrinsic to all large, complex organizations—even businesses and professions—since it is bureaucracy that permits smooth running, administratively efficient operations.[16] Every society needs things that are essential to its flourishing for which there is little economic incentive for their private production (highways, for example). The provision of such public goods and services, even if privatized at the final point of production (e.g., private contractors pour the concrete), usually occurs through a governmental or explicitly not-for-profit bureaucracy. Further, within bureaucracies, the worker is not the focal point, rather the efficiency of the productive process is the key concern (think of a state driver's license bureau). Traditionally, bureaucracies invest relatively little in their people, as the competencies needed for the routine and repetitive work processes designed for efficiency can be developed relatively easily in new workers.[17]

In contrast to both business and bureaucracy, a profession has as its central organizing feature the production of a unique type of work — expert work — which, by its very nature, the society cannot do for itself. Such work, far from being optional or nice-to-have, is fundamental to life and security and thus essential if the society is to flourish. Professional work requires years of education and apprenticeship before the aspiring professional can learn the theory and practice — the art — with which to serve society. The fields of medicine, theology, law, and more recently the military have traditionally been organized in western societies as a "social trustee" form of profession.[18] Effectiveness, not efficiency, is the key to the work of professionals — the sick want a cure, the sinner wants absolution, the accused want exoneration, and the defenseless seek security. To be sure, all clients in any professional field want efficient service, but effectiveness — truly efficacious results from the profession's expert practice — is their overriding goal. The service ethic of professions, whose responsibility is to the client rather than to self, is characterized as *cedat emptor*, "let the taker believe in us."[19] Clearly, the professional ethic is built on trust.

It follows that the means of motivation and social control within a profession — its ethic — is also quite distinct from those of business and bureaucracy. The client (i.e., the public in the case of the military) trusts the profession to produce the expert work when and where needed. And because of the client's trust in the professional's knowledge and practice, he/she is willing to grant significant autonomy to professionals to organize and police their own work. Thus, while businesses and bureaucracies traditionally motivate their workers by reliance on extrinsic factors such as salary, benefits, promotions, etc., professions in contrast use as means of social control largely intrinsic factors such as the privilege and honor of service, the satisfaction of nurturing and protecting life and enabling society to flourish, and the social status of membership in an old, honorable, and revered occupational group.

Further, it must be understood that professions, including the military, are quintessentially human institutions because of the nature of their productive processes. Specifically, after many long years of study and development, a professional practices his/her art by "the repetitive exercise of discretionary judgment," operating in areas where humanity's most profound concerns reside.[20] Think of even a junior-grade land combat professional leading a patrol in Baghdad. Over and over during the mission, he/she will make life-or-death decisions without reference to computers, doctrinal manuals, or written formulas, relying instead on the abstract knowledge about military operations he/she has gained through study and experience. Similar to the medical doctor in the clinic practicing the arts of diagnosis and treatment or to the lawyer researching and writing a case brief, military professionals may use advanced technology in many forms. But the essence of their practice is the human capacity to reason to efficacious decisions which, by their physical, intellectual, and moral character, they can then lead soldiers to implement.

The Role of Strategic Leaders of Military Professions.

Lastly, before returning to our discussion of dissent, we should note the unique role that strategic leaders, officers such as those in the general's revolt, have in the life of modern, competitive military professions. Their role mainly entails the maintenance of the right balance over time between the internal and external jurisdictions of the profession.[21] That is to say, in the profession's internal jurisdictions, creating expert knowledge and the development of professionals, the strategic leaders are responsible to see that, at any point in time, the profession has the expert knowledge needed to serve the client, and has embedded that knowledge into individual professionals and their units such that the profession can practice its art when and where the client might request it.[22] *As noted earlier, to maintain the client's trust in the profession's willingness and ability to serve the client effectively when and where service is required is the most fundamental moral obligation of a profession and, therefore, of its strategic leaders.* Sadly, after the fall of Baghdad in March 2003, it became apparent that previous and current strategic leaders of America's land combat professions, including the participants in the revolt, had failed conspicuously in that deep moral obligation, both to their collective client, the American people, and to their subordinates, who were asked to fight a counterinsurgency campaign with neither the expert knowledge nor the materiel support requisite to doing so.[23]

Within the two internal jurisdictions, and at only a slightly lower level of moral import, the central challenge for strategic leaders day-by-day arises from the fact that modern militaries by their design and character are both bureaucracy and profession! As summarized by one noted sociologist of the military:

> From the outset, the American military differed from other traditional professions *in always being practiced in a bureaucratic setting*, in being composed of people who in many cases did not have a lifelong commitment to their occupation, in having its autonomy constrained by responsibility to extra-professional (state) authority, and to explicitly being politically neutral (italics added).[24]

By the design and acts of many state legislatures and congresses over the decades, the military professions have been structured as a hierarchical, public-sector bureaucracy and have been treated as such all too often by those authorizing and sustaining such institutions.[25] Unfortunately, all too often the strategic leaders of our armed forces have responded by leading their institutions as bureaucracies, i.e., treating their soldiers as bureaucratic, civilian time servers, rather than as a proud breed of can-doers who march to an entirely different drummer.

Today's volunteers within our armed forces, particularly within the commissioned and noncommissioned ranks, volunteer with the intention and expectation of becoming professionals and being able to do their work in the physical environment and organizational culture of a profession–one that grants them significant autonomy to organize and execute their own work: "Professions are self-forming, self-regulating, and self-initiating in the provision of expert services to a client which the profession is ethically constrained not to exploit in its own self-interest."[26] In 2000, an Army major frustrated by the increasing bureaucratization of her chosen life's work put the question: "How can I be a professional if there is no profession?"[27]

The difficulty lies in the fact that leaders below the ranks of the colonels/captains and Flag Officers, who comprise the strategic leaders, have insufficient authority and capability to deflect the institution away from its bureaucratic pathologies and back to authentic professional practice. Recall again that the relationship between a profession and its client is one of trust, not of market forces, and that professions, unlike bureaucracies, rely for results on leadership and inspiration rather than managership and rule-mongering. Now, the challenge for strategic leaders in the military takes on new meaning!

No one can make our armed forces a profession rather than bureaucracy other than the uniformed strategic leaders, and even they must secure the cooperation of enlightened civilian leaders. One example of this immense responsibility is their control over the personnel development, evaluation and certification, assignment and utilization processes that will either motivate or demotivate aspiring professionals as they progress through a career of service. With significant autonomy already granted from civilian leadership, if the Army does not behave as a profession and develop inspired and competent professionals, it is because the strategic leaders have failed in their unique responsibility.

The Trust Relationships of a Profession's Strategic Leaders.

Let us now examine more closely the critical trust relationships that military professions hold and to which strategic leaders are parties. Each is deeply moral in content, reflecting the character of a dedicated profession. I posit that at a minimum there are three such relationships, and each can be qualitatively rated along a continuum ranging from "Fully Trusted" as the ideal to "Not Trustworthy" as the most opprobrious:[28] (1) the profession's relationship to the client, the American people; (2) the profession's relationships with the public's elected and appointed civilian leaders in both the Congress and in the Executive — the "civ-mil nexus" as it is becoming known.[29] This is a set of relationships inhabited by the strategic leaders of the military professions, both those on active duty and those retired (the "once a general, always a general" phenomenon of American political and military cultures); and (3) the relationship with subordinate leaders within the military professions, particularly the corps of commissioned and noncommissioned officers in our armed forces.

I will not spend much time defending these three as primary, as they flow largely from the foregoing discussion of the role and character of military professions in America. The first—the profession's relation to the American people—flows from the nature of "social trustee" professions and their service to their clients. The third — the profession's relation to subordinate leaders — is axiomatic to almost all the leadership doctrines of our armed forces — leaders at all levels serve their subordinates. The second relationship — the profession's relation to civilian leaders — may need a bit of explanation. It is derived from, and well-understood within, the literature and practice of American civil-military relations.

According to Samuel Huntington in 1957, and still very much accepted today, our military leaders have three responsibilities:[30]

(1) The representative function: "to represent the claims of military security within the state machinery."

I interpret and have experienced this to mean that officers are to express their expert point of view on any matter touching the creation, maintenance, use, or contemplated use of the armed forces. This point of view will derive from their years of formal education, training, and experience, a perspective not held by any other group, professional or otherwise, and without which informed public discourse and governmental policy formulation would be diminished.[31] This means officers are to represent forthrightly the military perspective in all forums, both in public view and out of view. Even Huntington was reluctant to draw explicit boundaries to the officer's responsibilities under this function. "The extent to which he may carry the presentation of his views is difficult to define, but he must recognize and accept the fact that there are limits."[32] Thus the behavior will depend on the personal discretion and professional judgment of the individual officer, as befits his/her role as a professional. Apparently, in the case of the generals' revolt, the officers construed the limits liberally, pressing their views even to the point of demanding an incumbent Secretary of Defense's resignation.

(2) The advisory function: "to analyze and to report on the implications of alternative courses of action from the military point of view." I understand this to mean the provision of candid professional military advice to elected and appointed civilian leaders, regardless of whether the advice was solicited or regardless of whether the advice is likely to be welcomed. Further, this means there is normally no legitimate role for uniformed officers in policy advocacy. Huntington considered such beyond their presumed competence.[33] The problematic nature of advice-giving by strategic leaders of military professions, especially under the

difficult conditions of being responsible to two often competing masters (Congress and Executive), are well-chronicled in the historical and civil-military literatures.[34] Even without the general's revolt, the Iraq War had heightened tensions at this civil-military nexus to a fever pitch with comments on the war's progress, or lack thereof, being instantly politicized by the news media, the administration, and the Congress.[35] Regardless, the professional responsibility is, and will remain, to render forthrightly such advice based almost solely on discretionary professional judgment. After that, the civilians must choose and decide. Regardless of the theorizing and hand-wringing of many academics and retired officers, there is simply no requirement that such advice be followed by the civilian leaders who receive it. Civilian leaders remain responsible to the electorate for any ill consequences of ignoring professional military advice and, of course, for all matters lying beyond the purview of their military advisors' issues such as the establishment of the political objectives of war and the assessment of political risk in its undertaking.[36]

(3) The executive function: "to implement state decisions with respect to state security *even if it is a decision which runs violently counter to his military judgment*" (italics added). Huntington's argument is quite to the point:

> The military profession exists to serve the state. To render the highest possible service the entire profession and the military force which it leads must be constituted as an effective instrument of state policy. Since political direction comes from the top, this means that the profession has to be organized into a hierarchy of obedience. For the profession to perform its function, each level within it must be able to command the instantaneous

and loyal obedience of subordinate levels. Without these relationships, military professionalism is impossible. Consequently, loyalty and obedience are the highest military virtues.³⁷

Today, few, if any, authorities disagree with the thrust of this argument.³⁸ Thus, for sound functional and instrumental reasons, the norm of the professional ethic is military obedience. What very narrow areas remain for military dissent, or even military disobedience, we shall return to later.

Factors for Evaluation of the Trust Relationships.

Given the functional activities for which the strategic leaders of our military professions are responsible, we can now evaluate the impact of potential acts of dissent on the three critical trust relationships. In broad terms, such moral relationships are always bilateral: profession and American people, profession and civilian leaders, and profession and junior leaders. We are interested here in how the other party in each bilateral relationship will perceive and understand the acts of dissent by the strategic leaders of the profession. Will they view the act as something that reinforces and builds trust within the relationship, or will they, on balance, construe the act as diminishing their trust in the leadership of the military professions and, thus, in the profession itself?³⁹

Therefore, completely apart from the legal, prudential, and substantive advisability of rendering a public dissent, strategic leaders must also consider the effects of the contemplated dissent on these precious bonds of trust between their profession and its clients. Such a moral analysis must address at least the following considerations:

- Gravity of the issue to the nation (and thus to the profession's client);
- Relevance of the strategic leader's professional expertise to the issue at hand (Does the issue fall squarely within the scope of the dissenters' expertise as a military professional?);
- Degree of sacrifice involved for the dissenter (Is the dissent motivated solely by a disinterested desire to serve the nation, even in the face of personal risk and sacrifice, or is there a self-serving subtext such as a desire to further one's own professional or political ambitions?);
- Timing of the act of dissent (Did the timing of dissent undercut the actions or policies being dissented from?); and,
- Congruency of the dissent with the prior, long-term personality, character, and belief patterns of the dissenter (Does the dissent strike a sudden discordant aberration from those authentic long-term behaviors that colleagues close to the dissenter would have expected?).

Such an analysis by a would-be dissenter could logically require 15 individual assessments, as shown in the matrix below, encompassing 5 factors analyzed for each of the 3 trust relationships. But in practice, some factors are obviously more salient than others. As I discuss each of these factors, a convincing case for the relative degree of importance I attach to each of them will become apparent.

(a) *Gravity of the Issue.* Wong and Lovelace are certainly correct: the gravity of the issue as regards the security of the Republic is a paramount factor in all three relationships. Logically, the higher the

	Trust with the American People	Trust with Civilian Leaders	Trust with Junior Leaders
Gravity of Issue			
Relevance to Expertise			
Degree of Sacrifice			
Timing of Dissent			
Authenticity as Leader			

stakes, the greater the temptation and justification will be for dissenters to speak out. There are two such understandings:

(1) The military professions serve solely to defend the Republic, which would otherwise be helpless and vulnerable. There is no raison d'être for the existence of military professions other than national security. If the security of the Republic is not in peril, there would appear to be no cause for military professionals to consider dissent.

(2) A second understanding is the inviolate principle of American civil-military relations the supremacy of civilian values and the concomitant subordination of the military to civilian leaders. Given this principle, how will acts of dissent with their inherent suggestion of insubordination be interpreted? The answer is not as straightforward as it might appear. Given a collective client deeply polarized along partisan lines, many of whom perceive the mil-

itary as too identified with the Republican Party and the current administration[40] and a war going badly over which the partisan divide is even deeper, what will be the perception of senior military officer dissent from decisions of that administration?

Recent research sheds some light on this issue. Though Huntington posited in 1957 the existence of a conservative military mind — an ideology that inheres in the professional function and which serves to restrain military involvement in politics and policymaking — it is the case that such does not exist to the same degree, if at all, today. Recent research shows quite clearly that, "Both in terms of their attitudinal pluralism and the shared liberal grammar employed to describe and justify their beliefs; the Army officers surveyed do not indicate any holistic attitudinal distinctions worthy of military-mind claims."[41] Thus, the recent dissent could well be construed as a positive development, suggesting that the putative military mind is not as monolithically partisan as argued by the academics and journalists. Whether this factor explains the revolt of high-ranking military officers against this administration, we cannot be sure.

Other scholars find that the public education aspect of such acts of dissent — military judgments about war, both in general and in its particulars — to be potentially very helpful in creating public discourse that is more fully informed. Without violating current limits on military participation in political activities, there are indeed several conduits through which military leaders can and do effectively make known expert information and policy preferences.[42] These include, in addition to their extensive access within the Executive branch, informal communications and meetings with members of Congress and their staffs; and dinners with journalists, business leaders, and other public figures. To agree with such political activity, one must accept military dissent as a form of negative advocacy that can be helpful to the functioning of the American political system. In view of senior officers' unique professional knowledge, that assertion is not questioned here. What is in question is how far dissent should be carried. For when dissent begins to shade over into political activity, or comes to be regarded as such, then the dissenters incur the risk of being seen as little more than uniformed lobbyists advocating a cause in behalf of their uniformed interest group — to the extreme detriment of both![43]

(b) *Relevance of professional knowledge and expertise to the issue in question.* Another important aspect of an act of dissent that will influence the perceptions of those in a trust relationship with the strategic leaders of military professions is the extent to which the issue falls within the leader's particular area of military expertise. In other words, why should the dissenter be listened to? By what expert knowledge and expertise is the credibility of the dissenter to be judged? If the issue does not fit within the compass of the profession's expertise, or only marginally so, one would expect observers to dismiss dissenters as free-lancers operating without standing, much as an Oscar-winning Hollywood actor who sets up shop as an authority on national defense. Strategic leaders speaking on matters beyond their professional military ken will likely be viewed as self-serving, using the status of their profession manipulatively to influence issue outcomes to their or their profession's advantage. A quicker way to rupture the moral relationships between profession and client can hardly be imagined!

Thus, we must be careful to understand the true essence of the issues that arise between civilian and military leaders, determining whether they are ⸢professional⸣ in some legitimate sense⸣ i.e., based on military expertise as derived from the art and science of war. If the issue can be thus characterized, then the professional is morally bound to ⸢profess⸣ (e.g., how many troops of what type are needed to support a particular war plan for a specific contingency, etc.). On the other hand, if the disagreements are based on the dissenter⸢s ⸢personal values and beliefs,⸣ that may go beyond the scope of his professional knowledge⸣ e.g., a personal belief that it is immoral to use an army in a manner that will ⸢break⸣ it, whatever that means to the individual strategic leader (the reader is encouraged to read again the second epigraph to this monograph).

We must also admit that parsing what is within the military⸢s knowledge and expertise is no easy task simply because the profession has done such a poor job of defining for itself such a knowledge map and establishing certification/licensure protocols that amplify for both military professionals and their clients what the boundaries are or should be. The only attempt by any military service to do this recently (the Army in 2002) revealed immense confusion on the part of the service and its strategic leaders, serving more than anything else to demonstrate why the service was contracting out various functions willy-nilly without any good understanding of future implications.[44] It was a case of a would-be military profession behaving almost purely as a bureaucracy.

That said, the potential dissenter must still decide; they must still use discretionary professional judgment to arrive at a decision to dissent. As Martin Cook has well-noted, the challenge is:

> ... how to understand professionalism so that two equal values, somewhat in tension with each other, are preserved: the unquestioned subordination of military of-

ficers to constitutionally legitimate civilian leadership; and the equally important role of the officer corps in providing professional military advice, unalloyed with extraneous political or cultural considerations.[45]

As Cook and others believe, part of that judgment must rest on the idea that professionals are obligated not only to serve the client (in this case, ultimately, the state and its constitution) but also obligated to have their own highly developed internal sense of the proper application of the professional knowledge.[46] In other words, dissent without insubordination to civilian authority can rightly be based on loyalty to the profession's expert knowledge and its appropriate application. If this were not the case, there would be no need for military professions—the Republic's security could be provided by businesses and bureaucracies.

Some scholars go even further. In a recent challenge to Huntington's functionalist assertion that loyalty and obedience are the cardinal military virtues, James Burk contends that:

> Military professionals require autonomy, to include moral autonomy, to be competent actors held responsible for what they do. By autonomy, I mean the ability to govern or control one's actions with some degree of freedom. Autonomous action is a precondition for responsible obedience and the opposite of blind obedience. . . . [There is a] conceptual space within which military professionals exercise moral discretion. The map includes a definition of responsible obedience and disobedience. But it also includes two types of actions that do not fit the classic definitions of these alternatives. They each exhibit a defect in which discretion is used either to do what is morally wrong or to do what was explicitly not authorized. Nevertheless, they are not simply forms of disobedience. They are "protected" actions, protected because the discretion to commit them preserves the au-

tonomy on which the moral responsibility of the military profession depends.⁴⁷

To me, Burk's argument is compelling. When the exercise of discretionary professional judgment leads to dissent, such acts by the profession's strategic leaders can fall in the "protected space" that professionals' actions occupy, a space that may indeed require acts of dissent or disobedience if "the moral responsibility of the profession is to be preserved," to again cite Burk. But that is a narrow space, indeed.

Knowing with certitude which acts fall in this narrow space will never be easy, but the knowledge that it exists should give both the professional and the client immediate pause when they hear assertions to the contrary as contained in the second epigraph to this monograph.

The last three factors to be considered in this moral calculus get to the motive of the dissenter. Since the other parties in these trust relations can never know a leader's innermost motives, they must rely on other indicators to inform them as to whether the dissenter's action is self-motivated or a act of selfless service as expected of a true professional. Such selfless motivation, as we have seen, reflects the core characteristic of the military profession and its members. The other parties of the trust relationship know this well, for it has long been understood that the military profession approaches ethical decisionmaking more from the perspective of virtue ethics than from a consequence- or rule-based philosophy:

> Thus, it is important to develop officers of character who understand what it means to be good officers—not just what it means to follow rules, perform duties, or reason well, although these are important to being ethical. . . . If

officers are to have the resources necessary to make ethically sound decisions, they need an approach to ethics that articulates what good character is, how it is developed, and how it influences moral decisionmaking.[48]

For insights into the motive of the dissenter, then, the other parties have at least three visible aspects of the public act to draw from: the degree of personal sacrifice involved for the dissenter, the timing of the act, and the apparent character of the dissenter.

(c) *Sacrifice incurred by the individual for taking the action.* Common sense must apply here, especially in the first and third relationships (the American people and junior professionals, respectively): the perceptions of the [other partner] to the trust relationship will be very strongly influenced by the degree of sacrifice incurred by the dissenter (loss of position, rank, active duty status, or even financial benefits in the case of resignation). In a profession that places great store in the military virtues of individual honor and loyalty up and down the chains of command, all members expect sacrifice to be a shared phenomenon at all levels; authentic leadership (equal risk-sharing) requires no less. For the true professional, a right understanding of one[]s loyalties always places loyalty to self dead last.[49] Thus, absent personal sacrifice, such dissent quickly leads to suspicion of and the search for ulterior motives (in the case of the revolt, political manipulation by the press and partisan political operatives who sought out the dissenters and arranged the interviews, placed their opinion editorials and arranged their television appearances, and grew the number of flag officers participating to six, etc.).

(d) *Timing of the Act of Dissent.* Here common sense must also apply. If something is worthy of an act of dissent, then it is worthy. Thus, as soon as that is discerned and decided by the strategic leader, the act should follow immediately. Any separation of months or years between the cause and the act is grounds, again, for suspicion of lack of moral agency and for a search for ulterior motives.

Again, this is particularly true in the third relationship. Junior military professionals expect their leaders to lead. The strategic leaders acting in dissent are the very same senior professionals who have taught and led in accordance with the profession's doctrines of decisiveness and audacity in battle; their subordinate followers will see no reason (nor will most Americans, I would suspect) for different qualities to apply in acts of dissent.

(e) *Authenticity as a leader.* Competent, ethically upright junior officers and noncommissioned leaders will go further toward shaping the future of the military profession and securing the Republic than any other part of the client base whose trust the profession must engender. To make these idealistic young professionals cynical about their calling, about their very futures and those of their families, is an unconscionably large price to pay for an act of dissent.

Over the course of long careers, not all strategic leaders in the military profession have displayed that steadfastness of character automatically assuring that any act of public dissent would be construed as disinterested. Yet the research shows that authenticity in leadership is crucial for a professional culture that engenders effective combat units.[50] Disillusionment occurs in junior officers and noncommissioned officers when they discover that the strategic leaders who have exhorted them on in combat turn out to have been opposed to the war for some time, or when they learn that they have risked their lives and those of their subordinates for a cause in which their leaders did not believe, even as they led. Such cynicism and lack of integrity in a senior leader is devastating to junior leaders at a very formative and vulnerable time in their careers. Assuredly, cynicism begets cynicism.

As research shows, in any hierarchical organization such as the military, there is always some amount of mistrust between junior professionals and their strategic leaders.[51] But in some periods, it becomes clearly excessive and destructive, as in the period surrounding the turn of the 20th century when the "exodus of Captains" occurred, a catastrophe in professional development from which the Army had not yet recovered when the Iraq War began.[52] Thus, the possibility of fomenting cynicism and the consequent exodus of younger professionals should always figure quite prominently in the calculation of those contemplating dissent.

PART III: CONCLUSIONS— SHOULD THERE BE FURTHER LIMITATIONS ON MILITARY DISSENT BY THE STRATEGIC LEADERS OF AMERICA'S MILITARY PROFESSIONS, PARTICULARLY THOSE IN RETIRED STATUS, OR IS THE CURRENT ETHIC, WHICH STRONGLY DISCOURAGES SUCH ACTS, STILL SUFFICIENT?

Vice Admiral James Stockdale, Vietnam prisoner of war and Medal of Honor recipient, once said, "even in the most detached duty, we warriors must keep foremost in our minds that there are boundaries to the prerogatives of leadership, moral boundaries."[53]

I have tried in this monograph to delineate a segment of these boundaries as they are understood from the study of military professions and as derived from the roles and responsibilities of those seniors privileged to be the profession's temporary stewards — the colonels/captains and Flag Officers who comprise the strategic leadership. Such boundaries mean that the decision to dissent can never be a purely personal matter. Rather it will reverberate outward impinging at a minimum the three critical trust relationships of the military profession — those with the American people, those with civilian and military leaders at the highest levels of decisionmaking, and those with the junior corps of officers and noncommissioned officers of our armed forces.

As we have seen, at least five different but closely related aspects of public dissent should be considered by the strategic leader when deciding whether to take such a step — the gravity of the issue; the relevance of the professional's expert knowledge and expertise to the issue at question; and, the three indicators of the dissenter's motive—the personal sacrifice to be incurred in dissenting; the timing of the act of dissent; and the congruence of such an act with the previous career of service and leadership within the military profession.

None of these five factors by themselves will likely be determinative for the would-be dissenter, but collectively they do provide a moral context and framework in which a judgmental decision should be made. If, as a result of these considerations, the military leader concludes that dissent is warranted — if the leader believes that an act of dissent best balances the immediate felt obligation to bring his/her professional military expertise to bear in a public forum with the longer-term obligation to lead and represent the profession as a social trustee, as a faithful servant of the American people, and as expressly subordinate to civilian control; then, in my judgment for those rare instances, there should be no additional restrictions placed on any act of dissent. On rare occasions, true professionals must retain the moral space to "profess."

Since the revolt just some 18 months ago, it is remarkable in retrospect how little it actually influenced events in the short term and how unremarkable it now appears from the vantage point of the mid term. The Republic, the war in Iraq, and the military profession proceed apace. And, as Lieutenant Colonel Paul Yingling's critique of the current state of "generalship" indicates,[54] the revolt may have contributed to an internal professional environment more open to honest dialogue and critique. If so, that is a positive development, indeed.

What remains now is for the strategic leaders of the military profession to strongly promote and follow the existing professional ethic, reinforcing a culture that discourages public dissent because of, as we have seen, the risks to the profession's essential trust relationships. One tentative attempt in this direction is a formal letter of guidance issued this fall by the new Chairman of the Joint Chiefs of Staff, Admiral Michael Mullen:

> To the degree we allow ourselves to disconnect from the American People, we allow the very foundation upon which our success rests to crumble.... Every action we take, every day, must be executed in a way that strengthens and sustains the public's trust and confidence in our ability and our integrity.[55]

This will be no easy task for the current leaders, but it is an urgent one—reasserting that they alone fulfill the functional roles of representing the profession, rendering advice, and executing legal orders. They must make it abundantly clear that they and they alone speak for the military profession. All other military voices, including those retired, are heard from nonpracticing professionals and should be considered as such. This will require reestablishing control over their profession's certification processes to ensure that all parties to civil-military relations understand that retired officers speak for no one other than themselves as citizens; and, most notably, that they do not speak for the current practicing professionals who now lead in America's conflicts.

As Admiral Stockdale noted, there are moral limits, but it is not clear to me that they have been ruptured by recent acts of dissent. However, they might be in the future, and at terrible cost to trust relationships, unless the profession's ethic on the rarity of public dissent is refurbished and fully implemented.

ENDNOTES

1. James A. Baker III and Lee H. Hamilton, co-chairs, *The Iraq Study Group Report*, December 2006, p. 52, available at *bakerinstitute. org/Pubs/iraqstudygroup_findings.pdf*.

2. Richard H. Kohn, "Huntington's Challenge: Maximizing Military Security *and* Civilian Control of the Military," chapter manuscript delivered at Senior Conference 07, United States Military Academy, West Point, NY, June 2007. Papers from the conference will be published in an edited volume in 2008.

3. Within the Army Profession, at least this moniker has become standard largely due to an article by former Chief of Military History Brigadier General John S. Brown, "The Revolt of the Generals," *Army* 56, September 2006, pp. 110-112.

4. As an example of the growing sharpness of this debate as it progresses, see the recent journal exchange by a number of respected academics, subsequently joined by former Chairman of the Joint Chiefs General Richard B. Myers in Michael C. Desch,

"Bush and the Generals," *Foreign Affairs*, Vol. 86, No. 3, May-June 2007, p. 97; and Richard B. Myers, Richard H. Kohn, Mackubin Thomas Owens, Lawrence J. Korb, and Michael C. Desch, "Salute and Disobey?" *Foreign Affairs*, Vol. 86, No. 5, September/October 2007, pp. 147-156.

5. Gregory Newbold, "Why Iraq was a Mistake," *Time*, Vol. 167, April 17, 2006, pp. 42-43.

6. The views of the six general officers can be found in many places in the journalistic literature. One good source is David Margolick, "The Night of the Generals," *Vanity Fair*, April 2007.

7. These concerns are central to Samuel Huntington's classic text, *The Soldier and the State*. See Samuel P. Huntington, *The Soldier and The State*, Cambridge, MA: Belknap Press of Harvard University Press, 1957, pp. 2-3.

8. The op-ed was accessed by the author on August 18, 2007, at *www.strategicstudiesinstitute.army.mil/pdffiles/PUB798.pdf*

9. I use the singular of "profession" in this text for simplicity, but the reader should know that there are, in fact, three military professions currently serving the Republic the aerospace military profession, the maritime military profession, and the land combat military profession and a fourth appears to be evolving. See Don M. Snider and Jeffrey Peterson, "Opportunity for the Army: Defense Transformation and the Emergence of a New Joint Military Profession," chapter 10 in Snider and Matthews, eds., *The Future of the Army Profession*, 2nd Ed., New York: McGraw-Hill, 2005, pp. 237-251.

10. For the most recent official discussion of the responsibility of Commissioned Officers, see Department of Defense, *The Armed Forces Officer*, Washington, DC: National Defense University Press and Potomac Press Inc., 2007.

11. Even so, those interested in the legal aspects should, at a minimum, see J. Mackey Ives, and Michael J. Davidson, "Court-Martial Jurisdiction over Retirees under Articles 2(4) and 2(6), Time to Lighten Up and Tighten Up?" *Military Law Review*, Vol. 175, March 2003, pp. 1-85, available at *www.loc.gov/rr/frd/Military_Law/Military_Law_Review/pdf-files/175-03-2003.pdf*.

12. See *Perspectives on Officership: The Commissioned Army Leader*, 3rd Ed., published by the William E. Simon Center for the Professional Military Ethic, United States Military Academy, New York: McGraw-Hill Publishing, 2005, p. xxxi; and *The Armed Forces Officer*, p. v.

13. For a more detailed presentation of the theory of modern professions applied to the Army, see Andrew Abbott, "The Army and the Theory of Professions," Chapter 24 in Don M. Snider and Lloyd J. Matthews, eds., *The Future of the Army Profession*, 1st Ed., New York: McGraw-Hill, 2002, pp. 223-236.

14. See Eliot Friedson, *Professionalism: The Third Logic: On the Practice of Knowledge*, Chicago: Univeristy of Chicago Press, 2001.

15. See Les Brownlee and Peter Schoomaker, "Serving a Nation at War," *Parameters*, Vol. 34, Summer 2004, pp. 4-23.

16. See Steven Brint, *In an Age of Experts: The Changing Role of Professionals in Politics and Public Life*, Princeton, NJ: Princeton University Press, 1994.

17. For an excellent, but short, comparison of bureaucracies and professions, see T. O. Jacobs and Michael G. Sanders, "Principles for Building the Profession: The SOF Experience," Chapter 20 of *The Future of the Army Profession*, 2nd Ed., pp. 441-462.

18. For major recent works on professions, see Andrew Abbott, *The Theory of Professions*, Chicago: University of Chicago Press, 1998; and Eliot Freidson, *Professionalism Reborn: Theory, Prophecy and Policy*, Chicago: University of Chicago Press, 1994.

19. David Segal and Karen DeAngelis, "Changing Conceptions of the Military Professions," chapter manuscript delivered at Senior Conference 07.

20. Don M. Snider, "The Multiple Identities of the Army Officer," Chapter 6 in *The Future of the Army Profession*, 2nd Ed., p. 143.

21. See Leonard Wong and Don M. Snider, "Strategic Leadership of the Army Profession," Chapter 28 in *The Future of the Army Profession*, 2nd Ed., pp. 601-624.

22. I am using the singular of client here for simplicity of argument and presentation. As I will develop later in this monograph, the strategic leaders of military professions actually serve multiple clients: first, they serve the soldiers they lead who are the sons and daughters of the American people; second, they serve their military and civilian superiors who direct the profession with delegated authority from the American people; and third, ultimately, they serve the people themselves for whom they are providing security.

23. I say "previous and current" since it takes 5-10 years to create new expert knowledge and develop its use in leaders and their units up to battalion level. Thus, our land combat forces today are the product of the strategic leadership that held stewardship over these professions in the 1990s and the early part of this decade.

24. See Segal and DeAngelis.

25. One need only think of the micro-detail in the annual authorizing and appropriations processes of congressional subcommittees to recognize the truth of this statement.

26. See Jacobs and Sanders, pp. 441-462.

27. See Gayle L. Watkins and Randi C. Cohen, "In their Own Words: Army Officers Discuss Their Profession," Chapter 5 in *The Future of the Army Profession*, 2nd Ed., pp. 115-138.

28. One interesting fact flowing from the study of professions is that the strategic leaders of military professions today do not get to determine if their institution is a profession or not. This is always the prerogative of the client, in this case the American public. If one does not believe that the client can determine for itself that the military is not a profession, one need only recall the years after Vietnam, or the loss of autonomy imposed on the Navy after the Tailhook incident or on the Army after the training scandal at Aberdeen.

29. See Christopher Gibson, "Enhancing National Security *and* Civilian Control of the Military: An Argument for a Madisonian

Approach," chapter manuscript delivered at Senior Conference 07.

30. Huntington, *The Soldier and The State*, pp. 72-73.

31. My own experience chairing interagency meetings while on the staff of the National Security Council, The White House, 1987-89, confirmed the accuracy of this understanding.

32. See Huntington, *The Soldier and The State*, p. 72.

33. *Ibid.*

34. See Lloyd Matthews, "Army Officers and the First Amendment," *Army*, January 1998, pp. 31-32.

35. For a superb account of the influences on administration decisionmaking before and during the Iraq War, see Michael R. Gordon and Bernard E. Trainor, *Cobra II: The Inside Story of the Invasion and Occupation of Iraq*, New York: Pantheon Books, 2006.

36. See Suzanne C. Nielsen, "The Rules of the Game: The Weinberger Doctrine and the American Use of Force," Chapter 10 in *The Future of the Army Profession*, 1st Ed., pp. 199-224.

37. See Huntington, *The Soldier and The State*, p. 73.

38. Indeed, one respected scholar concludes: "The law is now generally understood to require that soldiers resolve all doubts about the legality of a superior's orders in favor of obedience." Mark J. Osiel, *Obeying Orders: Atrocity, Military Discipline and the Law of War*, Brunswick, NJ: Transaction Publishers, 1999, p. 5.

39. A major premise to the analysis in this section is that a leader's actions, including those of dissent, do influence the trust component of their relationships with those they both serve and lead. I do not think this point needs further elaboration.

40. See Ole R. Holsti, "On Chasms and Convergences: Attitudes and Beliefs of Civilians and Military Elites at the Start of a New Millennium," Chapter 1 in Peter D. Feaver and Richard H. Kohn, eds., *Soldiers and Civilians: The Civil-Military Gap and*

American National Security, Cambridge, MA: Belfer Center for Science and International Affairs, Harvard University, 2001, pp. 15-100.

41. See Darrell W. Driver, "The Military Mind and the Military Profession: A Reassessment of the Ideological Roots of American Military Professionalism," chapter manuscript delivered at Senior Conference 07.

42. See Risa Brooks, "Rethinking Subjective Control: Political Activity of the Military in Democracies," chapter manuscript delivered at Senior Conference 07.

43. See Richard H. Kohn, "Military and Civilian Behaviors to Maximize National Security and Assure Civilian Control," chapter manuscript delivered at Senior Conference 07.

44. See Richard Lacquement, "Mapping Army Professional Expertise and Clarifying Jurisdictions of Practice," and Deborah Avant, "Losing Control of the Profession Through Outsourcing?" Chapters 9 and 12, respectively, in *The Future of the Army Profession*, 2nd Ed., pp. 213-236, 271-290.

45. See Martin Cook, *The Moral Warrior: Ethics and Service in the U.S. Military*, Albany: State University of New York Press, 2004, pp. 55.

46. *Ibid.*, p. 65.

47. See James Burk, "Responsible Obedience and Discretion to Do What is Wrong," chapter manuscript delivered at Senior Conference 07.

48. See Tony Pfaff, "The Officer as Leader of Character: Leadership, Character, and Ethical Decision-Making," Chapter 6 in Snider and Matthews, eds., *The Future of the Army Profession*, 2nd Ed., pp. 153-161.

49. See George M. Clifford III, "Duty at All Costs," *Naval War College Review*, Vol. 60, No. 1, Winter 2007, pp. 103-128.

50. See Patrick J. Sweeney and Sean T. Hannah, "High-Impact Military Leadership: The Positive Effects of Authentic Moral

Leadership on Followers," Chapter 4 in Don M. Snider and Lloyd J. Matthews, eds., *Forging the Warrior's Character: Moral Precepts from the Cadet Prayer*, Sisters, OR: Jericho LLC, 2007, pp. 127-162.

51. See Walter F. Ulmer and Joseph J. Collins (Project Directors), *American Military Culture in the Twenty-First Century*, Washington DC: Center for Strategic and International Studies, 2000, pp. xv-xxvii.

52. See Mark Lewis, "Transformation and Junior Officer Exodus," *Armed Forces and Society*, Fall 2004, pp. 63-93.

53. Quoted by General Peter Pace, Chairman, Joint Chiefs of Staff, in the Introduction to the *Armed Forces Officer*, p. ix.

54. See Paul Yingling, "Failure in Generalship," *Armed Forces Journal International*, May 2007.

55. Michael G. Mullen, "CJCS Guidance for 2007-2008," letter dated October 1, 2007, available at *www.jcs.mil/CJCS_GUIDANCE.pdf*.

Made in the USA
Lexington, KY
28 October 2018